MAKING THINGS CHANGE

© Aladdin Books Ltd 2010

Published in the United States in 2010 by
Stargazer Books, distributed by
Black Rabbit Books
P.O. Box 3263
Mankato, MN 56002

Illustrator: Tony Kenyon

Printed in the United States

Library of Congress Cataloging-in-Publication Data

Gibson, Gary, 1957-
  Making things change / Gary Gibson.
      p. cm. -- (Fun science projects)
  Includes index.
  ISBN 978-1-59604-190-5
  1. Science--Experiments--Juvenile literature. 2. Scientific recreations--
Juvenile literature. I. Title.
  Q164.G522 2009
  507.8--dc22

                              2008016397

Fun Science Projects

MAKING THINGS CHANGE

GARY GIBSON

Stargazer Books
Mankato, Minnesota

CONTENTS

INTRODUCTION

Things around us are changing all the time. Many things we come across in our lives change their size, shape, color, and even their chemical or physical state. But how and why does it happen? How can a flower change its color? Why does warm water rise? Why do some cars rust? This book contains a selection of exciting "hands-on" projects to help answer some of these questions.

When this symbol appears, adult supervision is required.

GET AN ADULT TO DO THIS FOR YOU

FREEZING AND MELTING

When the weather becomes cold, it can change many of the things around us. It can cause water to freeze, or solidify, into ice or snow. This change is easy to reverse; warmed ice will thaw, or melt, back into water.

EXPANDING ICE

1 Find two large empty plastic bottles. Tape a paper marker around each about halfway up.

2 Using a large pitcher of water, carefully fill each of the bottles exactly to the mark on the paper.

3 Place one bottle in a warm room and the other in your freezer. Leave them overnight.

4 Take out the frozen bottle and compare the water level in each of them.

WHY IT WORKS

There seems to be more ice. This is because water expands, gets larger, when it freezes. Pipes sometimes burst in winter because the water inside freezes and expands.

FURTHER IDEAS
Find lumps of chocolate, butter, and wax from a candle, about the same size as an ice cube. Place them on a tray. Leave the tray in a warm place to compare how they melt. Place the tray in the freezer to reverse the changes.

THE ACID TEST

Chemicals are split into families of *acids, alkalis,* or *neutrals.* These chemicals are everywhere—even in soil. The color of the Hydrangea flower depends on the levels of acid or alkali in the soil. Blue flowers mean there is more acid in the soil; pink, more alkali.

MAKE A CHEMICAL INDICATOR

1 Take a red cabbage, tear it into shreds, and place these shreds into a bowl.

GET AN ADULT TO HELP YOU WITH THIS

2 Pour hot water into the bowl. The cabbage color dissolves to make an indicator.

3 Strain the juice, and pour the liquid into three small jars.

WHY IT WORKS

A chemical that changes color in acids and alkalis is called an indicator. Red cabbage juice turns red when in acids, like vinegar, and green when in alkalis, like soap.

4 Add a different liquid to each jar, such as vinegar or liquid soap. Compare the colors.

FURTHER IDEAS
Make indicator paper by soaking blotting paper in the indicator. Then test household chemicals.

9

BUBBLES AND FIZZ

Carbon dioxide is the gas in carbonated drinks which keeps them full of bubbles. When you shake a carbonated drink, then suddenly release the cap, the gas inside bubbles up and escapes. Carbon dioxide gas is important in other ways. It can be used to put out fires and it also makes cakes rise. Here you can make your own bubbles of gas.

MAKE AN ERUPTING VOLCANO

1 Find a small glass jar. Stand it on a saucer. This will be your volcano.

2 Cover the sides of the jar with clay to make the volcano.

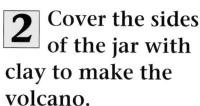

3 Carefully fill half the jar with baking soda. Add a few drops of red food coloring. Then add vinegar, a spoonful at a time.

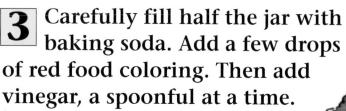

4 Stand back and watch as the mixture bubbles up and over the sides of the volcano.

WHY IT WORKS

A mixture of the acid in vinegar and alkali in baking soda makes bubbles of gas. The thousands of bubbles are very light and this causes the mixture to fizz. The eruption of bubbles is similar to lava erupting from a volcano.

FURTHER IDEAS
Fill a glass with vinegar and add a tablespoon of baking soda. Drop in mothballs. Bubbles of gas make them rise back to the surface.

PRETTY FLOWERS

Plants, like animals, need water to stay alive. The roots of plants are especially good at taking water from the ground. Water moves through the plant in tiny tubes that are similar to the blood vessels in an animal.

CHANGE FLOWER COLORS

1 Fill three glass bottles with water. Add a few drops of different food coloring to each.

2 Find three freshly cut flowers, preferably white or light-colored.

3 Trim the stem of each flower before placing them into the three bottles.

4 Leave the flowers overnight. Each becomes the color of the water in which it was placed.

WHY IT WORKS

Water travels up the stem of each flower and spreads to all parts of the plant, including the petals. The water then escapes from the plant into the air by evaporation. Fresh water is continually drawn up to replace the lost water.

FURTHER IDEAS

Repeat with a fresh stalk of celery. When the water has risen through it, ask an adult to slice the stalk. With a magnifying glass you should see the thin tubes that carry the water.

FLOWING CURRENTS

Currents of hot air rise from warm valleys to the cooler hilltops. These are called *thermals*. They are very useful to hot air balloons, gliders, and even birds. The rising warm air helps to keep them aloft.

SEE HOT WATER CURRENTS

GET AN ADULT TO DO THIS FOR YOU

1 Find a small jar with a metal screw-on lid. Ask an adult to make some small holes in the lid.

2 Tie a piece of string tightly around the neck of the jar. Make sure the string can support the jar.

3 Place a few drops of food coloring in the jar and fill it with hot water. Screw the lid on tightly.

4 Fill a glass pitcher with cold water. Holding the string, gently lower the glass into the pitcher.

5 Watch as the colored water swirls around in the cold water.

WHY IT WORKS

Hot liquids expand and become less dense than the cold liquid around them. This causes the hot liquid to rise into the pitcher. Eventually the heat is spread out, and the cooled, denser liquid sinks to the bottom of the pitcher. This movement of the liquid is known as a *convection current*.

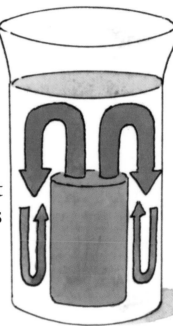

FURTHER IDEAS
Cut out some strips from circles of paper. Hold them above a heater. Rising warm air causes the strips to rotate.

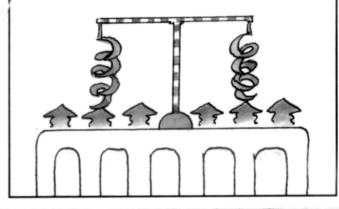

RISING TEMPERATURES

On a hot day, you can see the temperature rise if you watch a thermometer carefully. As the air gets hotter, the liquid inside the thermometer expands up the glass tube. All liquids expand when heated, but usually only by a tiny amount.

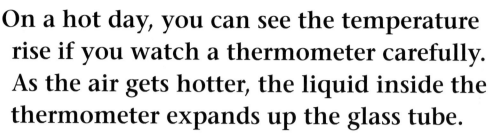

GET AN ADULT TO HELP YOU WITH THIS

MAKE A BOTTLE FOUNTAIN

1 Find a small glass jar with a screw-on lid. Fill the jar half full with cold water. Add a few drops of food coloring.

2 Ask an adult to make a hole in the lid just big enough for a thin straw. Seal the straw in place with some clay.

3 Plug the end of the straw with clay. Use a pin to make a tiny hole in the plug.

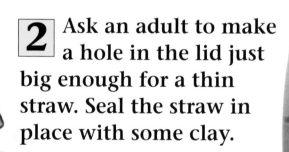

4 Fill a large bowl with hot tap water. Stand the small jar upside-down in the bowl on some clay, with the straw sticking above the water level.

WHY IT WORKS

The heat from the hot water bowl warms up the air inside the jar, and this air expands. As it does so, it pushes on the water below. The water can only escape one way—by spraying out of the top of the straw.

5 Wait for the small jar to heat up, and stand back to admire the fountain of colored water spraying out of the top.

FURTHER IDEAS
Fill a jar with water. Put a straw through a hole in the lid and seal with clay. Turn the jar upside-down. See how the level in the straw changes when the jar is put in hot water and in a refrigerator.

SEPARATING MIXTURES

Tap water has been filtered many times to remove all impurities before you drink it. Filtering is like straining; it is a way of purifying a liquid by removing any solids that do not dissolve naturally.

MAKE MUDDY WATER CLEAR

1 Mix some mud, clay, or soil with water in a jar. Make a cone shape out of a coffee filter.

2 Carefully place the cone in the neck of a clean glass jar. Slowly pour the muddy mixture through the cone.

3 See how much clearer the filtered water appears. Warning: Do not drink the filtered water—it still contains germs.

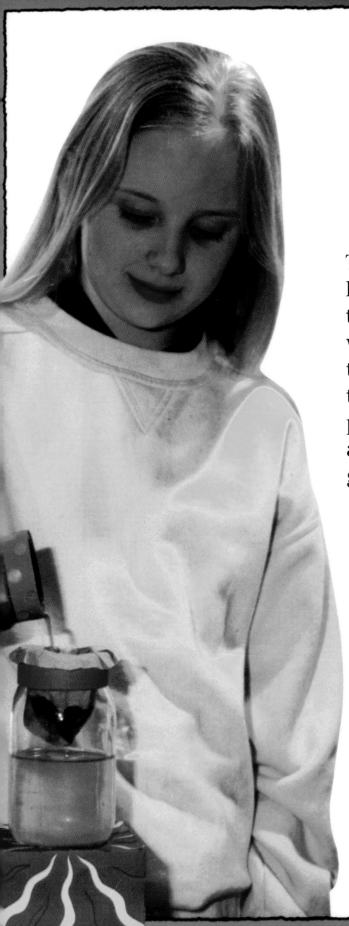

There are tiny holes in the paper that only allow water droplets to squeeze through. The pieces of solids are larger and get trapped.

FURTHER IDEAS

Dissolve some salt in a tall, clean glass of water. Leave it in a warm place for a few days. See how the salt is left behind when all the water has evaporated.

RUST OR BUST

Though many metals are strong, tough materials, they do not last forever. When iron is constantly damp it will rust; pieces of iron turn brown and crumble away. Rust can be a terrible problem. It can attack your car, bicycle, or anything else made from iron. The iron is changed into a new chemical that we call rust, or "iron oxide."

A RUST RACE

1 Set up five glass jars with some steel wool in each. Add nothing to the first jar. Fill half the second jar with tap water. Fill the third to the brim with boiled water and tighten the lid. In the fourth, put the steel wool on a piece of damp cloth. Put tap water in the last jar, and add a pinch of salt.

2 Leave the jars for at least a week. Regularly examine the steel wool for signs of rust.

WHY IT WORKS

So-called "steel wool" is really made of iron. The steel wool rusts in jars 2 and 4, but especially in jar 5. Iron needs water and air to rust. The air and water particles attach to the iron particles to form iron oxide. Boiled water has no air in it. Salt makes iron rust faster.

FURTHER IDEAS
Scratch away some of the surface of some empty cans. See if the cans rust when damp.

INVISIBLE INK

Have you ever wanted to write a secret message that only you can read? This project lets you write your message on a sheet of paper. When you have finished, the message is invisible—the paper just looks blank. Nobody can read it unless they know the method for making the message visible.

SEND A SECRET MESSAGE

1 Squeeze some lemon juice into a glass.

2 Dip a paintbrush into the juice and draw your picture onto white paper. Let the paper dry completely.

3 Ask an adult to place the paper in the oven for a few minutes, and the picture will reappear.

GET AN ADULT TO DO THIS

WHY IT WORKS

When the lemon juice is heated, water evaporates away. The compounds that remain combine with oxygen in the air. This turns the juice brown and makes the picture visible.

FURTHER IDEAS
Draw on white paper using a wax candle. Warm the paper on a radiator until the wax melts and the picture is revealed.

SPLITTING COLORS

If you look very carefully with a magnifying glass at the colored dots that make up the colors in this book, you may notice that there are only four colors. All of the other colors are made by mixing these colors together.

SEPARATE COLORED INKS

1 Cut some blotting paper into strips, 1 in (2.5 cm) wide and 6 in (15 cm) long.

2 Make a large dot just above the bottom of each strip with several different-colored felt-tip pens.

3 Tape the other end of the strips to a string. Hang the string over a bowl with two pencils set in clay. Fill the bowl with water until it touches the strips.

4 Watch the water rise halfway up the strips. Remove them, and see how the colors have separated.

WHY IT WORKS

The inks are made from different colors, e.g. green is made from blue and yellow. These are separated by the rising water because some travel through the paper faster than others.

FURTHER IDEAS
Mix some food colorings. Repeat the experiment with one drop of this mixture and watch the colors separate.

BURNING AND BREATHING

Air is really a mixture of many gases. Most of the air is made up of nitrogen. One fifth is made up of oxygen. Oxygen is needed for fires to burn and for people to breathe. Without oxygen, people would suffocate and die.

INVESTIGATE A BURNING CANDLE

1 Use clay to stand a candle upright in the middle of a small, shallow saucer.

2 Place four piles of coins around the clay so that a jar can sit over the candle.

3 Add a few drops of food coloring to a pitcher filled with water. Then fill the saucer with the colored water.

WHY IT WORKS

4 Ask an adult to light the candle and lower the jar over it. Watch the water level in the jar rise as the candle goes out.

GET AN ADULT TO DO THIS

The burning candle flame uses up the particles of oxygen. Water is sucked up into the jar to replace the used oxygen. Water rises about one fifth up the jar. The burning stops when all of the oxygen in the jar has been used up.

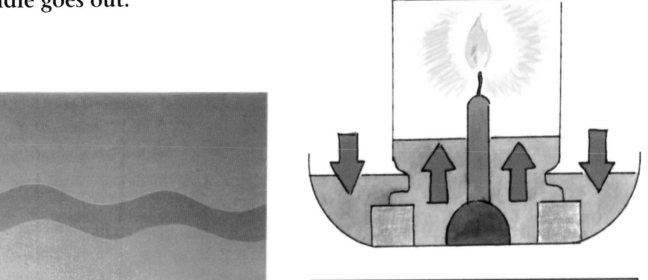

FURTHER IDEAS
Compare how similar candles burn when different jars are placed over them. The longer they burn, the more oxygen is present.

LIVING YEAST

Most germs, or "microbes," are bad for us, because they cause illness and disease. However, some microbes can be useful to us. We use microbes to make yogurt, cheese, bread, and beer. Yeast is a microbe that looks like a yellow powder, but under a microscope you can see that it is made of living cells.

SEE YEAST BREATHING

1 Find a glass bottle and pour in a teaspoonful of sugar and some dried yeast.

2 Pour in some warm water. Swirl the bottle to mix the water, sugar, and yeast.

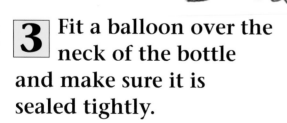

3 Fit a balloon over the neck of the bottle and make sure it is sealed tightly.

4 Stand the bottle in a large bowl of hot water to keep it warm. Watch the mixture for bubbles of gas. Eventually, the balloon will fill with gas and inflate.

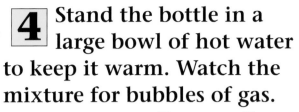

WHY IT WORKS

When you add the warm water, the yeast "wakes up" and feeds on the sugar. As it feeds, it breathes out carbon dioxide and fills the balloon.

FURTHER IDEAS

Stir a spoonful of sugar and dried yeast in warm water. Mix 8 oz (227 g) of flour with ½ oz (14 g) of butter and a little salt. Add the yeast and water and knead into a dough. Bake the bread for fifteen minutes at 425°F (220°C).

FANTASTIC CHANGE FACTS

The hottest temperature ever recorded was a scorching 136.4°F (58°C) in the sands of Al'Aziziyah, Libya. At the other end of the scale, Vostok in Antarctica experienced a frigid –136.4°F (–89.2°C), to become the coldest place on Earth.

In November 1956, a massive iceberg was spotted in the South Atlantic Ocean. It measured 208 miles (335km) long and 60 miles (97km) wide and covered over 12,000 square miles (31,000 square km)—larger than the state of Massachusetts!

Chameleons can change their skin color in response to the light around them. They can range from green, yellow, or white one minute, and then brown, or even black the next.

Butterflies completely change from their early caterpillar state. The largest butterfly is the Queen Alexandra's birdwing which measures 11 inches (280mm).

Puffer fish are able to expand their body like a balloon to twice their normal size by swallowing water. They do this to protect themselves from other fish that may want to eat them.

The tallest fountain in the world can be found at Fountain Hills in Arizona. At full power the column of water can spout up to 625 feet (190m) in the air.

Your stomach contains powerful acids and enzymes that turn the food you eat into a souplike mush that your body can absorb.

The largest loaf of bread ever baked was made in Johannesburg, South Africa. It weighed nearly one and a half tons, and was 10 feet (3m) long.

Salt pans are areas of countryside that are covered in a layer of dazzling white salt. They are formed when water in a lake evaporates, leaving behind the salt that used to be dissolved in it.

GLOSSARY

Acid
A class of substances that turn vegetable indicators (e.g. litmus) red. Many occur naturally; hydrochloric acid is found in the stomach and helps food digestion.

Alkali
A class of substances that turn vegetable indicators green.

Cell
The basic structure found in a living organism. A human body is made up of millions of these tiny "building blocks."

Convection currents
Circular movements in fluids caused by warm substances rising, cooling, and then falling again.

Filter
A process to purify substances by removing impurities.

Freeze
When a substance turns from a liquid into a solid as its temperature drops.

Indicator
Shows the chemical condition of a substance by changing color. Litmus turns red for acids, green for alkalis, and blue for neutrals.

Melt
To change from a solid to a liquid when the temperature rises.

Microbe
A microscopic living organism.

Molecule
The smallest particle of a substance that still has the substance's properties. A molecule may contain several atoms.

Oxidize
To combine a substance with oxygen.

Temperature
The level of heat that a body has. It is measured in degrees of Celsius, Fahrenheit, and Kelvin.

Thermal
An ascending current of warm air.

INDEX